For all portable keyboards *by Kenneth Baker.*

THE COMPLETE KEYBOARD PLAYER

BOOK 3

£3.95
W

About this book, 3

Wise Publications

Exclusive Distributors:
Music Sales Limited
8/9 Frith Street, London W1V 5TZ, England
Music Sales Pty. Limited
120 Rothschild Avenue, Rosebery, NSW 2018, Australia

This book © Copyright 1984 by
Wise Publications
UK ISBN 0.7119.0596.7
UK Order No. AM 38324

Music Sales complete catalogue lists thousands of
titles and is free from your local music book shop,
or direct from Music Sales Limited.
Please send £1 in stamps for postage to
Music Sales Limited, 8/9 Frith Street, London W1V 5TZ.

Printed in England by
Halstan & Co. Ltd., Amersham, Bucks.

ABOUT THIS BOOK

In Book Three of The Complete Keyboard Player you learn about scales and keys. When you play in different keys you make basic changes of sound, and so add a new dimension to your playing. Minor keys, especially, can change the whole flavour of your music. In Book Three you play in five new keys, including two minor keys.

In Book Three you continue your left hand studies, with the emphasis as usual on "fingered" chords. Nine new chords are introduced, in easy stages, and all the chords used in the series appear in the Chord Chart at the back of the book.

There is plenty for your right hand in Book Three. There are double notes, chords, fill-ins, counter-melodies, and so on, and several new and effective tricks of the trade, such as ornamental "grace notes" and acciaccaturas.

As usual, throughout the book you will get tips on how to use the facilities of the keyboard — the sounds, the rhythms, and so on — more effectively.

Although Book Three continues in the "teach yourself" tradition of the earlier books, all teachers of the instrument will want to make it one of their standard text books.

CHORD OF E7

1

Using single-finger chord method:

Locate "E" (the higher one of two) in the accompaniment section of your keyboard. Convert this note into "E7" (see Book One, p. 42ff., and your owner's manual).

Using fingered chord method:

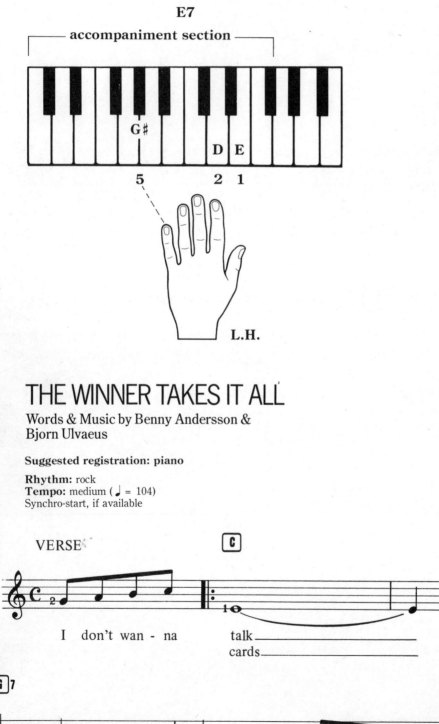

E7

accompaniment section

G♯   5

D   2

E   1

L.H.

THE WINNER TAKES IT ALL

Words & Music by Benny Andersson & Bjorn Ulvaeus

Suggested registration: piano

Rhythm: rock
Tempo: medium (♩ = 104)
Synchro-start, if available

VERSE

C

I don't wan - na   talk _____   a - bout things we've
cards _____   and   that's what you've

G7   Dm

gone   through _____   though it's hurt - ing   me _____
done   too _____   no - thing more to   say _____

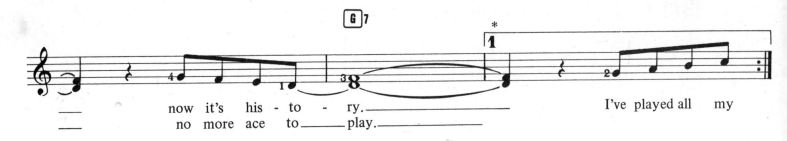

now it's his - to - ry._____ I've played all my
no more ace to ____ play._____

*1st Time Bar. Play this bar on the first time through only (then repeat as marked).

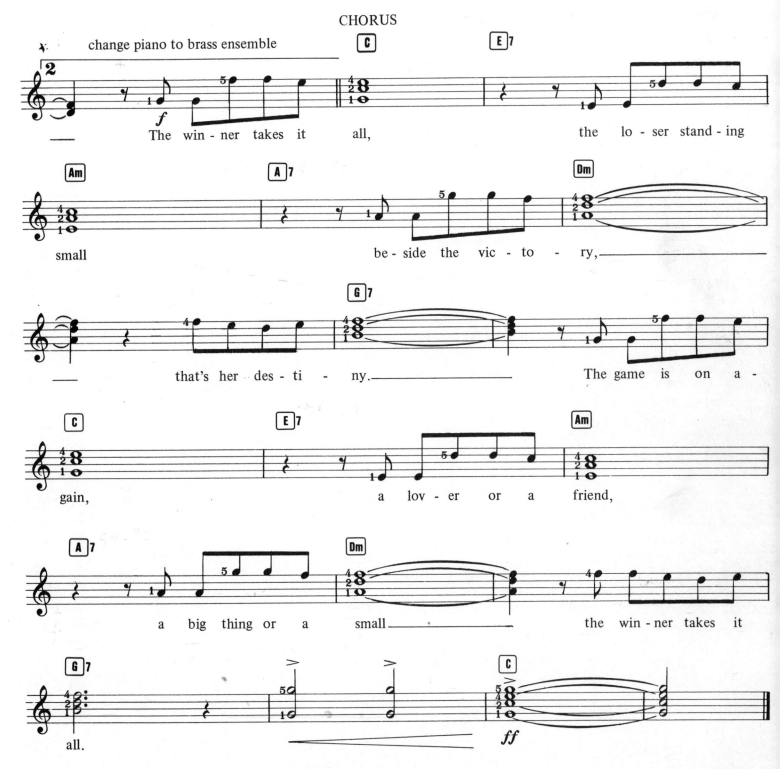

CHORUS

change piano to brass ensemble

The win - ner takes it all, the lo - ser stand - ing

small be - side the vic - to - ry,_____

that's her des - ti - ny._____ The game is on a-

gain, a lov - er or a friend,

a big thing or a small_____ the win - ner takes it

all.

✱ 2nd Time Bar. Play this bar on the second time through only (then carry on to the end).

I LEFT MY HEART IN SAN FRANCISCO

Words by Douglas Cross
Music by George Cory

Suggested registration: string ensemble

Rhythm: swing
Tempo: fairly slow (♩ = 88)
Synchro-start, if available

air, I don't care! My love waits there

___ in San Fran - cis - co.

A - bove the

blue

and wind - y sea.

When I come home to you, San Fran -

cis - co.

Your gold - en sun will

shine for me.

CHORD OF E MINOR (Em)

2 Using single-finger chord method:

Locate E (the higher one of two) in the accompaniment section of your keyboard. Convert this note into "Em" (see Book Two, p.28, and your owner's manual).

Using fingered chord method:

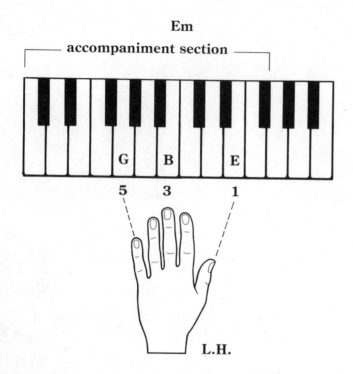

Em

accompaniment section

BRIGHT EYES
Words & Music by Mike Batt

Suggested registration:
electric guitar + arpeggio

Rhythm: rock
Tempo: medium (♩ = 96)

VERSE

Is it a kind of a dream._____
fog a-long the ho - ri - zon.

Float - ing out on the tide._____
Cold sound in the air._____

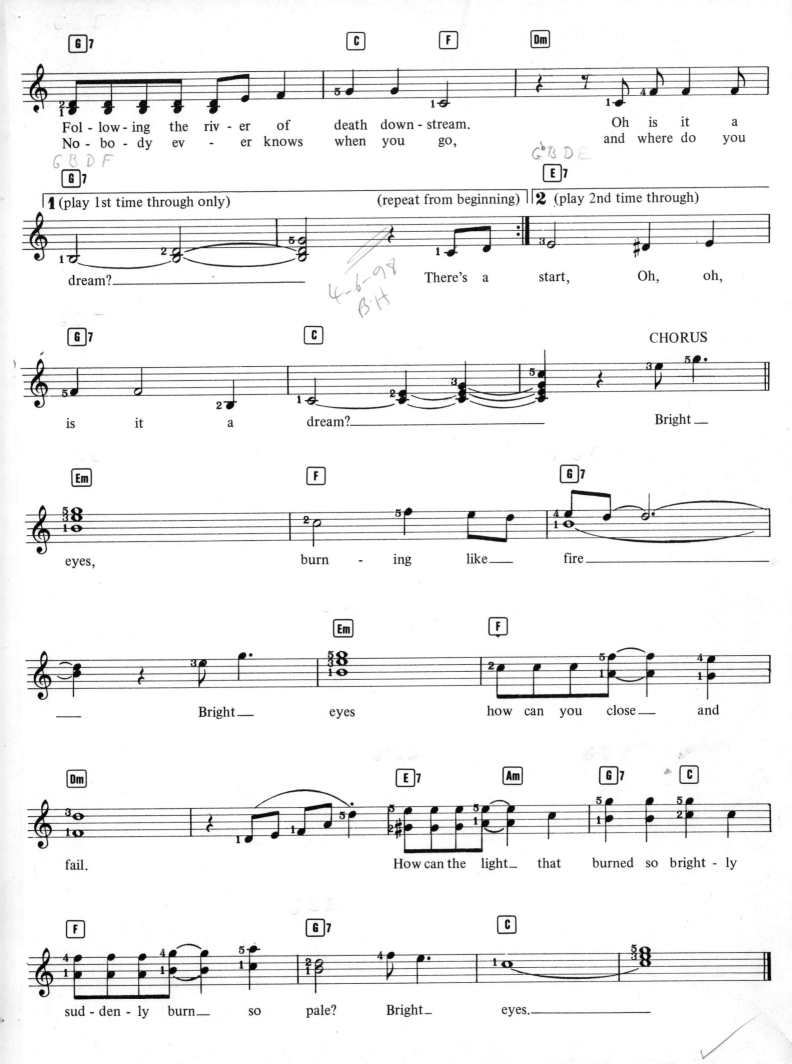

THE SONG FROM "MOULIN ROUGE"

(WHERE IS YOUR HEART?)

Words by William Engvick
Music by Georges Auric

Suggested registration: hawaiian
guitar

Rhythm: waltz
Tempo: slow (♩ = 80)
Synchro-start, if available

When - ev - er we kiss, I

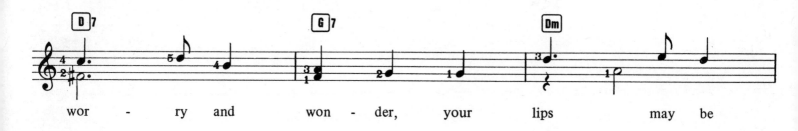

wor - ry and won - der, your lips may be

here, but____ where is your heart? It's

al - ways like this, I wor - ry and

won - der, you're close to me here, but____

*split these two notes (playing lower note
first).

10

where is your heart? It's a sad thing to re-al-

ise that you've a heart that nev-er melts. _____ When we

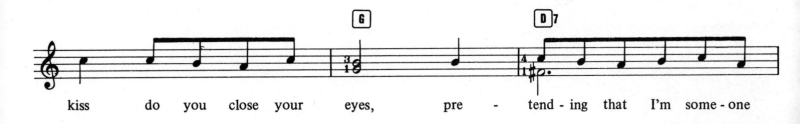

kiss do you close your eyes, pre-tend-ing that I'm some-one

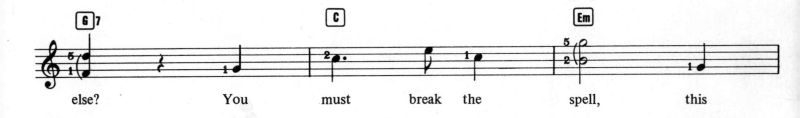

else? You must break the spell, this

cloud that I'm un-der, so please won't you

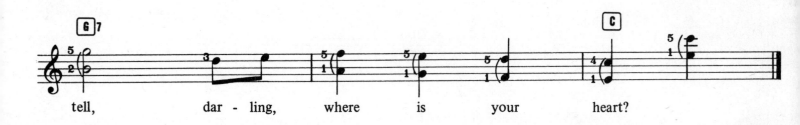

tell, dar-ling, where is your heart?

SCALE OF C; KEY OF C

3

A scale is a succession of adjoining notes:

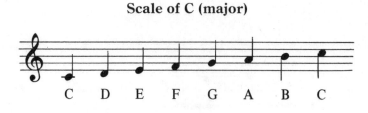

Scale of C (major)

C D E F G A B C

As you see, there are no black notes in the scale of C.

When a piece is built on this scale it is said to be in the "key of C". Almost all the pieces you have played so far have been in the key of C. The occasional black notes you encountered in those pieces were of a temporary nature only, and did not affect the overall key.

From now on you are going to play in a number of different keys for the sake of contrast.

SCALE OF F; KEY OF F

4

Scale of F (major)

F G A Ⓑ♭ C D E F

As you see, a B Flat is required to form the scale of F. When you are playing in this key, therefore, you must remember to play all your B's, wherever they might fall on the keyboard, as B Flats.
To remind you, a B Flat is inserted at the beginning of every line:—

key signature

To help you further, I have arrowed the first few B Flats in the following songs.

CHORD OF B♭ ; CHORD OF F7

5 You need these two chords in order to play in the Key of F.

Using single-finger chord method:

Locate "B♭" in the accompaniment section of your keyboard. Play this note on its own and you will have a chord of B♭ (major).

Locate "F" (the lower one of two) in the accompaniment section of your keyboard. Convert this into "F7" (see Book One, p. 42ff., and your owner's manual).

Using fingered chord method:

B♭

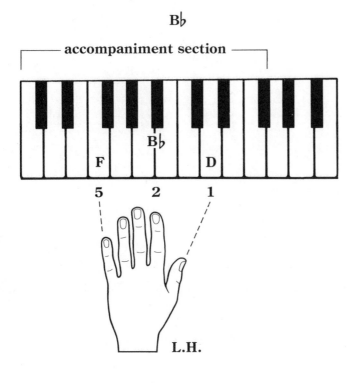

F7

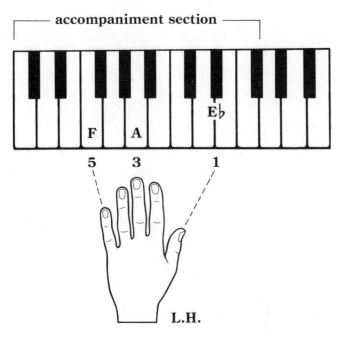

OB-LA-DI, OB-LA-DA

Words & Music by John Lennon & Paul McCartney

Suggested registration: funny

Rhythm: swing
Tempo: fast (♩ = 112)

* Cut Common Time. A feeling of two in
a bar (**2/2**) rather than four (**4/4**). Notice the
metronome marking: ♩ = 112.

TIME ON MY HANDS

Words by Harold Adamson & Mack Gordon
Music by Vincent Youmans

Suggested registration: string ensemble

Rhythm: swing
Tempo: slow (♩ = 84)

Time on my hands.

You in my arms. No-thing but love _____ in view. _____

Then if you fall, once and for all,

I'll see my dreams _____ come

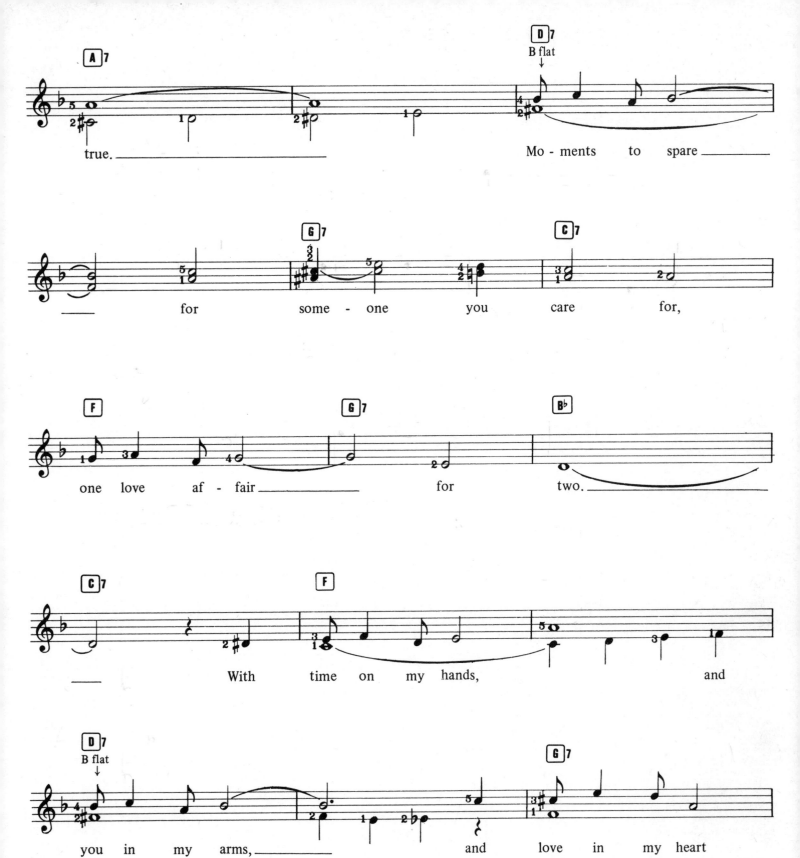

TULIPS FROM AMSTERDAM

English Words by Gene Martyn
Original Words by Neumann and Bader
Music by Ralf Arnie

Suggested registration: accordion

Rhythm: waltz
Tempo: fast (♩ = 184)
Synchro-start, if available

When it's spring a - gain, I'll bring a - gain Tu - lips from Am - ster - dam. With a heart that's true I'll give to you Tu - lips from Am - ster - dam. I can't

wait un - til the day you fill

these emp - ty arms of mine. Like the

wind - mill keeps on turn - ing, that's how

my heart keeps on yearn - ing, for the

day I know we can _____ share these

Tu - lips from Am - ster - dam.

SIXTEENTH NOTES (SEMIQUAVERS), AND DOTTED RHYTHMS

6 An eighth note (quaver) can be
subdivided into two sixteenth notes
(semiquavers):-

eighth note   sixteenth notes

A dotted eighth note is equal to half as
much again (see "dotted time notes",
Book Two, p. 29), that is, three sixteenth
notes:-

dotted eighth note   sixteenth notes

In practice a dotted eighth note usually
pairs up with a sixteenth note:-

dotted eighth note   sixteenth note

Together, these two time notes are
equivalent to 4 sixteenth notes, or 1
quarter note (crotchet):-

3 sixteenth notes + 1 sixteenth note = quarter note

The general effect of a passage like:-

is of eighth notes (quavers) with a "lilt".

The phrase "humpty dumpty" is a useful guide to this rhythm:-

say: Hump-ty Dump-ty Hump-ty Dump-ty

stress   stress   stress   stress

These uneven types of rhythms are often called Dotted Rhythms.
Look out for dotted rhythms in the next four pieces.

SCALE OF G; KEY OF G

7

Scale of G (major)

G   A   B   C   D   E   (F♯) G

An F Sharp is required to form the scale of G. When a piece is built on this scale it is said to be in the "key of G". When you are playing in this key you must remember to play all F's, wherever they might fall on the keyboard, as F Sharps. The key signature, which appears at the beginning of every line, will remind you:-

key of G

key signature

YELLOW SUBMARINE

Words & Music by John Lennon & Paul McCartney

Suggested registration: piano

Rhythm: swing
Tempo: medium (♩ = 100)
Synchro-start, if available

*Triplet. A triplet is a group of 3 notes played in the time of 2. These three eighth notes (quavers) must be played slightly faster than normal eighth notes, in order to fit them into the bar.

CHORD OF B7

8

Using single-finger chord method:

Locate "B" in the accompaniment section of your keyboard. Convert this into "B7" (see Book One, p. 42ff., and your owner's manual).

Using fingered chord method:

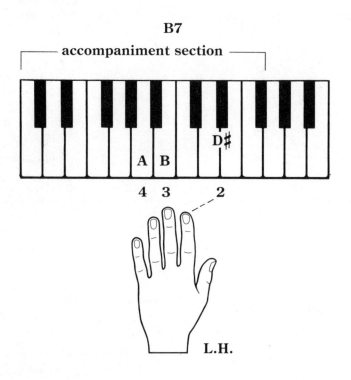

B7

CHANSON D'AMOUR
Words & Music by Wayne Shanklin

Suggested registration: clarinet

Rhythm: swing
Tempo: medium (♩ = 100)

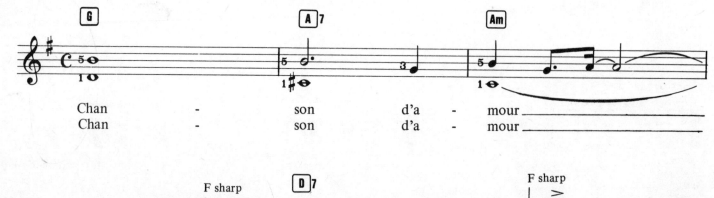

Chan - son d'a - mour _____
Chan - son d'a - mour _____

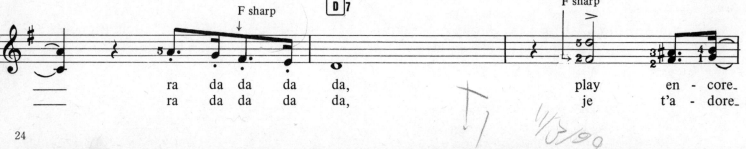

ra da da da da,   play   en - core
ra da da da da,   je   t'a - dore

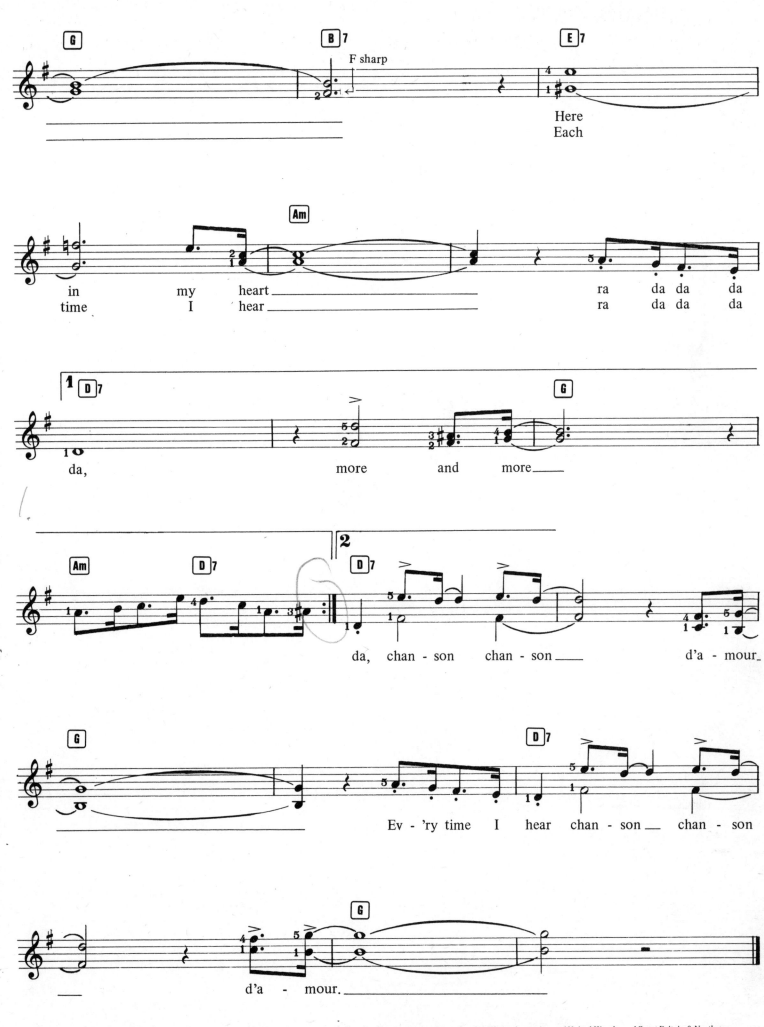

WHEN I'M SIXTY-FOUR

Words & Music by John Lennon & Paul McCartney

Suggested registration: funny +
              duet (if available)

Rhythm: swing
Tempo: medium (♩ = 108)
Synchro-start, if available

When I get old - er, los - ing my hair __ ma - ny __ years from

now, will you still be send - ing me a Val - en - tine __

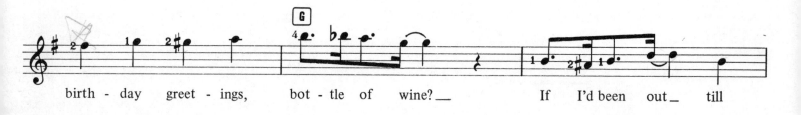

birth - day greet - ings, bot - tle of wine? __ If I'd been out __ till

quar - ter to three __ would you lock the door?

Will you still need __ me, will you still feed __ me, when I'm six - ty __

CHORDS OF G MINOR (Gm), AND B♭ MINOR (B♭m)

9

Using single-finger chord method:

Locate "G" and "B♭" in the accompaniment section of your keyboard. Convert these notes into "Gm" and "B♭m"

respectively (see Book Two, p. 28, and your owner's manual).

Using fingered chord method:

Gm

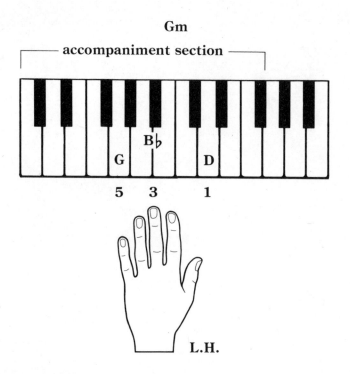

Compare this chord to G (major), a chord you already know.

B♭m

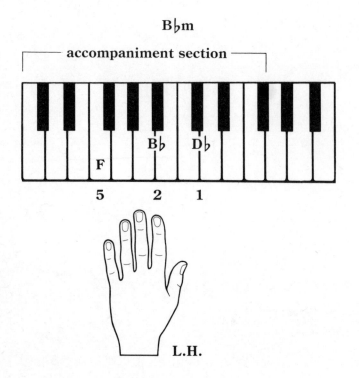

Compare this chord to Bb (major), a chord you already know.

ISN'T SHE LOVELY
Words & Music by Stevie Wonder

Suggested registration: piano +
sustain

Rhythm: swing
Tempo: medium (♩ = 112)
Synchro-start, if available

*Quarter Note (Crotchet) Triplet. 3 quarter notes played in the time of 2. Play these quarter notes slightly faster than usual, in order to fit them into the bar, but keep them even, and equal to each other.

DREAM LOVER

Words by Clifford Grey
Music by Victor Schertzinger

Suggested registration: violin
solo

Rhythm: waltz
Tempo: medium (♩ = 84)

Dream lov - er fold your arms a - round me, Dream lov - er, your ro - mance has found me. I'm held in your spell, know - ing too well dreams nev - er tell _____

*Acciaccatura. A purely ornamental note, not included in the timing of the bar. Play the acciaccatura note as quickly as possible.

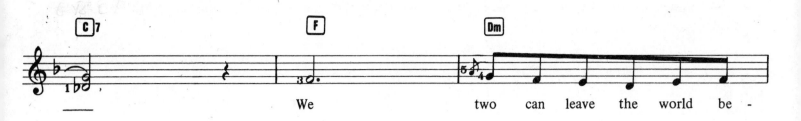

We two can leave the world be-

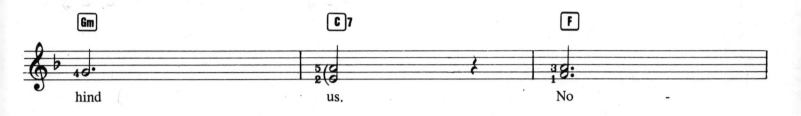

hind us. No -

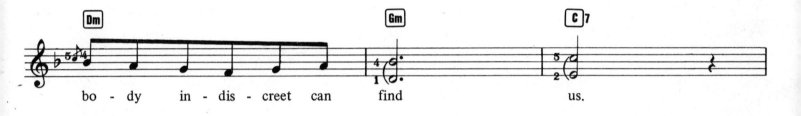

bo - dy in - dis - creet can find us.

Dream lov - er of mine,

se - crets di - vine I am shar - ing with

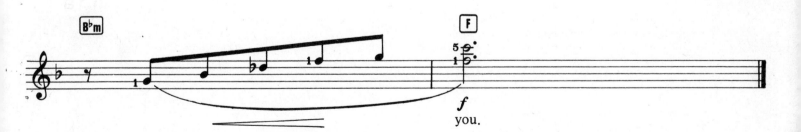

you.

f

MINOR KEYS

10

So far almost all your playing has been in major keys: C, F, and G. Songs written in minor keys, with their preponderance of minor chords, often have a sad, nostalgic quality, which makes an excellent contrast.

KEY OF D MINOR

11

The key of D Minor is related to the key of F Major. The scales on which these keys are built use the same notes:

scale of D Minor

D E F G A (B♭) C D

scale of F

F G A (B♭) C D E F

All the notes are white except one: B Flat. As you would expect, both keys have the same key signature:

key of D Minor

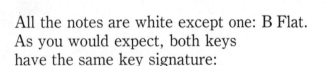

key of F

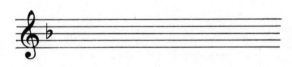

When playing in the key of D Minor (as in the key of F), you must remember to play all B's, wherever they might fall on the keyboard, as B Flats.

SUNNY

Words & Music by Bobby Hebb

Suggested registration: jazz organ,
with stereo chorus.

Rhythm: rock
Tempo: medium (♩ = 96)

Sun - ny   yes - ter - day my life   was   filled with

rain. _____   Sun - ny   you smiled at me and

real - ly eased the   pain, _____   oh the dark days are done   and the

bright days are here,   my Sun - ny one shines   so sin - cere, _ oh, Sun - ny one so

true,   I love   you. _____ f f

HAVA NAGILA

Traditional

Suggested registration: clarinet
Rhythm: march $\frac{2}{4}$ (or swing)
Tempo: medium ($\quarternote$ = 88)

* Grace Notes. Purely ornamental notes
not included in the basic timing of the
bar. Play your grace notes as quickly as
possible.

KEY OF E MINOR

12
The key of E Minor is related to the key
of G Major. Both keys use the same scale
notes:

scale of E Minor

E F♯ G A B C D E

scale of G

G A B C D E F♯ G

All the notes are white except one:
F Sharp.

The key signature is the same for both
keys:

key of E Minor

key of G

When playing in the key of E Minor (as
in the key of G), you must remember to
play all F's, wherever they might fall on
the keyboard, as F Sharps.

TABOO

Words by S. K. Russell
Spanish words & music by Margarita Lecuona

Suggested registration: clarinet

Rhythm: tango
Tempo: medium (♩ = 116)

Slow - ly _____ the East - ern moon as - cend - ed _____

Night came _____ and found her close be -

side me.

FINE

Al - though I knew this was mad - ness.

Mere - ly a pre - lude to sad - ness.

D.C. al Fine

ANNIVERSARY SONG

Words & Music by Al Jolson & Saul Chaplin

Suggested registration: violin

Rhythm: waltz
Tempo: quite fast (♩ = 160)

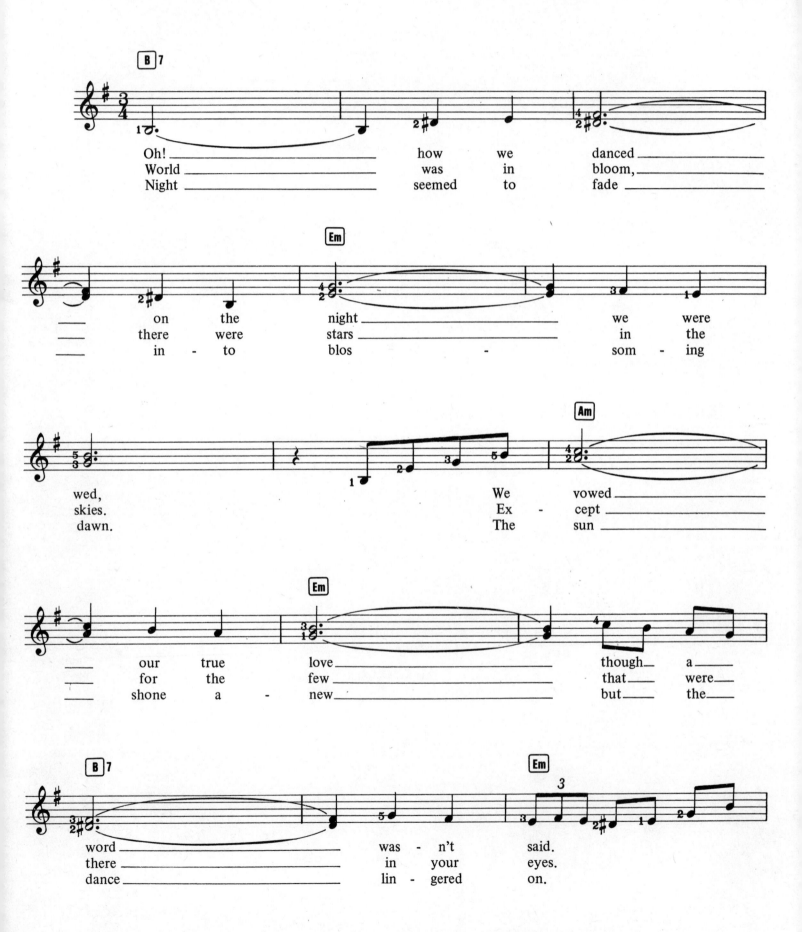

The

Dear, as I

held you so close in my arms.

An - gels were sing - ing a hymn to your

charms. Two hearts gent - ly beat - ing were

mur - mur - ing low: "My dar - ling I

D.C. al Fine
accordion to violin

love you so!" The

KEY OF B FLAT

13

The scale of B Flats, and therefore the key of B Flat, requires two flats: B Flat, and E Flat:—

scale/key of B Flat (major)

key signature

Bb C D Eb F G A Bb

When you are playing in this key you must remember to play all B's and E's, wherever they might fall on the keyboard, as B Flats and E Flats, respectively.

CHORD OF Eb (MAJOR)

14

Using single-finger chord method:

Play the note "Eb" (the higher one of two) in the accompaniment section of your keyboard.

Using fingered chord method:

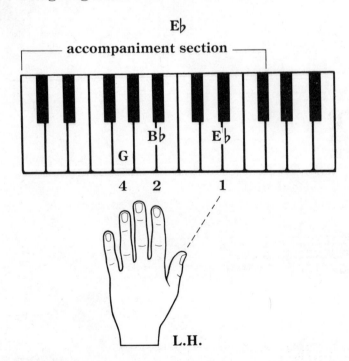

Eb

accompaniment section

G   Bb   Eb

4   2   1

L.H.

DON'T CRY FOR ME ARGENTINA

Music by Andrew Lloyd Webber
Lyrics by Tim Rice

Suggested registration: Trumpet

Rhythm: tango
Tempo: medium (♩ = 112)

Don't cry for me Ar - gen - ti - na, the truth is I nev - er left you. All through my wild days, my mad ex - ist - ence, I kept my pro - mise, don't keep your dis - tance. _____ Don't cry for me Ar - gen - ti - na, the truth is I nev - er left you. All through my wild days, my mad ex - ist - ence, I kept my pro - mise, don't keep your dis - tance. _____

Change Trumpet to Clarinet

MAMMA MIA

**Words & Music by Benny Andersson, Stig Anderson &
Bjorn Ulvaeus**

Suggested registration: synth. guitar

Rhythm: rock
Tempo: medium (♩ = 126)

VERSE

I've been cheat-ed by you___ since I don't know when.
So I made up my mind___ it must come to an end.

Look at me now___ will I ev-er learn?

I don't know how___ but I sud-den-ly lose___ con-trol

There's a fire___ with-in my soul___ just a

look and I can hear a bell ring___ One more look and I for-get ev-'ry-thing___

15

Using single-finger chord method:

Locate "C" (the higher one of two) in the accompaniment section of your keyboard. Convert this note into "Cm" (see Book Two, p. 28, and your owner's manual).

Using fingered chord method:

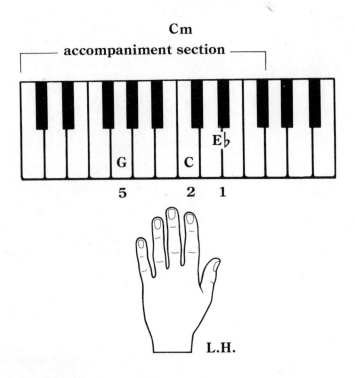

Compare this chord to C (major), a chord you already know.

RAINDROPS KEEP FALLING ON MY HEAD

Words by Hal David
Music by Burt Bacharach

Suggested registration: electric guitar

Rhythm: Swing
Tempo: medium (♩ = 104)

Rain - drops   keep fall - in' on   my   head,
did   me   some talk - in' to   the   sun.

TELSTAR

By Joe Meek

Suggested registration: jazz organ,
    with tremolo

Rhythm: disco
Tempo: medium (♩ = 120)

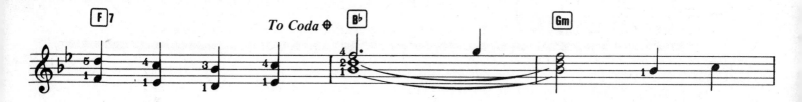

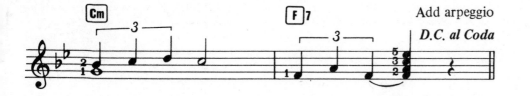

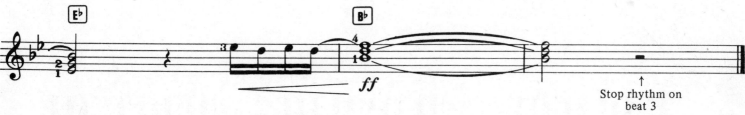

CHORD CHART (Showing all "fingered chords" used in the course)

C
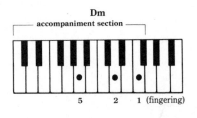

Cm
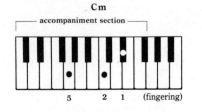

C7
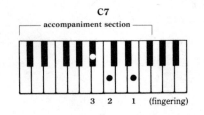

Dm
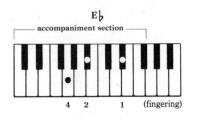

D7
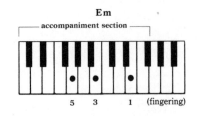

E♭
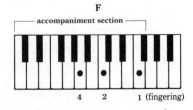

Em
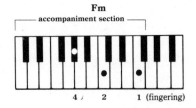

E7
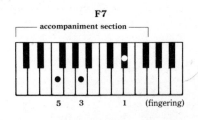

F
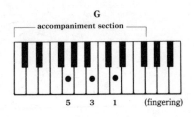

Fm
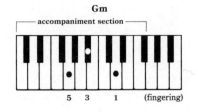

F7
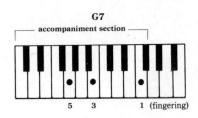

G
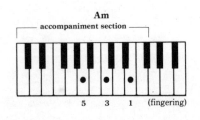

Gm
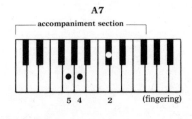

G7
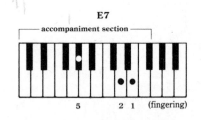

Am
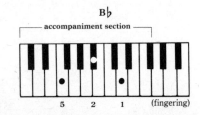

A7
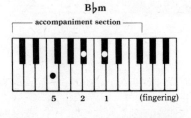

B♭
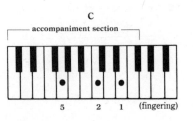

B♭m
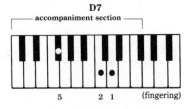

B7
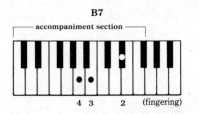